I WANT MORE

Honouring God's Servant Gives Me More

THELMA PORTER

2017

THE PUBLISHER'S NOTEBOOK LIMITED

THE PUBLISHER'S
NOTEBOOK LIMITED
PUBLISHERS FOR THE CHRISTIAN GENRE

I WANT MORE: *Honouring God's Servant Gives Me More*

ISBN: 978-976-96123-4-1

Cover Art: Dale Sewell

Publisher: The Publisher's Notebook Limited

Lot 376, 8 West, Greater Portmore

St Catherine, Jamaica

Telephone: (876) 782-1866

Email: thepublishersnotebook@gmail.com

publisher@thepublishersnotebook.com

DEDICATION

- This book is dedicated to:

- You who are engaged in a spiritual search because you want more. You are not satisfied with where you are
- You who know there's something more but are not sure of ways to get more

- You who are connected to a Servant of God and have the desire to honour this Servant but are not quite clear on how to do so

- You who are connected to a house of worship but never realized that honouring God's Servant is also honouring God

- You who are just curious about what honouring a Servant of God entails

CONTENTS

FOREWORD

I take pleasure in my child in applauding her in writing this book. **(Psalm 149:4)**; **(Psalm 147:11)**. I rejoice over her effort with gladness **(Zephaniah 3:17)**

I have known her all her life **(Genesis 2:7)**; in fact, I knew her even before she was formed **(Psalm 139:16)**. I was the architect of her very substance in her mother's womb **(Psalm 139:13)**; and therefore, I even know the number of hairs on her head **(Luke 12:7);(Matthew 10:30)**.

We have such an intimate relationship that I know what she is going to say before she says it; and I know how she thinks **(Psalm 139:2, 4)**. In my Kingdom, she is valuable **(Matthew 10:31)**; and because I knew she would be called; from beginning I gave her dominion and power over the works of my hands **(Psalm 8:6)**. She holds a very important place and position in my Kingdom; and as she writes about the importance of honour, I have already glorified and honoured her **(Psalm 8:5)**:- honour begets honour.

She is my handiwork who I've given the skill to do this work. **(Ephesians 2:10; Exodus 35:10)**Wouldn't I therefore know her competence and capability? This book shall serve great people **(Proverbs 22:29)** including you. I therefore have absolutely no doubt that her book will add value to the lives of those who read it

> Jehovah God
> Creator of the Universe

i

PREFACE

Do you have a yearning desire for MORE? MORE in terms of wealth, better health, better job, success on the job, debt reduction, debt cancellation, better relationship with your children, better relationship with your spouse, successful children? Do you want more in terms of wisdom, knowledge and understanding; the fruit of the Spirit, clarity, direction from God, major breakthroughs? The answer lies in your Honour: honour to God; and to His servants, especially His Chief Servant. This book is about how honouring God's Chief Servant can enhance your life in such a way that you live a life of success and never lack. It's a Kingdom principle.

In I Want MORE, my intention is to help you to realize how one phenomenon, like honouring God's Servant, can enhance not just yours but the lives of your family members and the people with whom you are associated. You wanting MORE can be the catalyst for a major life changing experience. Ask yourself two questions; Am I where I want to be in life? Do I want MORE? If you answered "No" and "Yes" respectively, you are on the right track. There is always more. You were wired that way! Jesus himself said you will be able to do greater things than he did (John 14:12)

I Want MORE will encourage you. It will assist you. It will enhance your life. It will set you up for major breakthroughs and it will prepare you to become your life changer.

ACKNOWLEDGEMENTS

To:

• God Almighty, the Creator, for His leading on and direction in my life

• Bishop Courtney McLean and WAFIF- Worship and Faith International Fellowship for the inspiration given from the worship experience (being in the atmosphere)

• John Maxwell, celebrated author; for his confirmation, through non personal means, albeit from afar, that I should do this.

• Aisha Porter-Christie; my beautiful and blessed daughter, for her support and for understanding the reason I had to do this

INTRODUCTION

Here I am writing a book. This is not the first attempt. I've written a book for students preparing for the Common Entrance Exam that gave rise to the current exit exam – the Grade Six Achievement Test (GSAT) which will soon be changed to the Primary Exit Profile (PEP). That is still in manuscript form after decades. I have been told, in a prophetic word, to take it off the book shelf and dust it off; and that I will do. I also wrote a text for one of the literacy courses at the University of the West Indies. That has since been revised by someone else because I didn't have the time to do the revision; or I should say, didn't make the time to do it; so my authorship for the current text is null and void.

So, what makes this book different? Two reasons. First; I have been given some tools for writing which should also be the standard for everyone who aspires to write. The tools come from one of the best authors in the business; John Maxwell (who has written more than 80 books to date and has sold millions).

John Maxwell states that a writer must 'live the message' being written about. According to him, "If you don't live it, don't write it." He says a writer must 'know the message." "If you don't know it, don't write about it." Finally, "Know your audience; the success of how well your book is received, is going to be based on the audience you've written for." Thank you, John Maxwell; With God's help, I have been working hard at living my message; I know my message and I know the audience for whom I'm catering. I'm catering to everyone who loves the Lord and are striving to do His will; I'm writing for those who have been toiling hard in the vineyard and who still yearn for more; as well as those who have not got to that stage as yet, but will soon, by the fervent prayers of their loved ones; by intercessors who constantly stand in the gap; and by God's will. So, that includes you who are now reading this.

This great author also said that the question on writing a book should not be, "Do I want to write a book?" but rather, "Do I have a big idea; do I have a great thought that needs to be passed on to others?" Well I do. It might not be unique but it means wonders to me having come into the newness of being really excited about God, of having fun with worshipping Him and having a hunger for more and to follow hard after God like David as he stated in Psalm 63:8 (KJV).

My second reason for this book being different is that I am writing under an anointing. I am writing out of honour. I am writing out of obedience. I am so blessed now and so in love with the Lord in a different way; and at a higher level; that when I sensed that it was God's Spirit who moved me to write this book, I had to obey.

This book is a picture of who I am becoming. I hope to continue writing. I believe that as I write, other opportunities and ideas will come. It is my hope that what is coming from me will add value to your life; and that it will be a motivating factor for your personal and spiritual development.

May you be convicted by the Holy Spirit; may your heart be stirred as you turn each page; and may you be tremendously blessed.

I WANT MORE

Honouring God's Servant Gives Me More

1. The Beginning....

I stepped into Worship and Faith International Fellowship (WAFIF) for the first time on December21, 2014. It's a ten minute journey from my home. I believe it was an Act of God. It was a Sunday and I was on my way to celebrate with a friend at the church he pastored; he was due to do his last sermon before leaving the island. However, that was not God's plan – "For I know the plans I have for you," says the Lord. "They are plans for good...to give you a future and a hope." (Jeremiah 29:11 NLT).

While journeying, I got a call and received some disturbing news about this pastor friend. My spirit became troubled; and I decided immediately not to complete this journey. I'm sure it would have been fine to go to that church on that day; but God had plans for my future and so the stage had to be set that Sunday in December.

Just at the time I got the disturbing news and made my decision, I had reached Old Harbour Road and the entrance of the road to WAFIF; I made that left turn; a turn which was to have an impact on the rest of my life....

My knowledge of Worship and Faith International Fellowship started through LOVE 101 FM; a radio station in St. Andrew, Jamaica. My radio dial was on that frequency at 4:45 one morning. I woke to a programme called 'Miracles Now' and I remember being fascinated by the preaching. Honestly, I didn't remember the title of the sermon or the preacher's name but I remembered hearing something which fed my soul and spirit at that time. I heard the programme again and made note of the name of the worship centre – WAFIF. The interesting thing was that the address was given as Old Harbour Road which intrigued me because that was a route I plied daily. I decided to be intentional and look out for WAFIF during my daily journey. I didn't find the place and then forgot about it.

Lo and behold, one evening on my way home, there it was; a directional sign with the huge letters- WAFIF. I made note of it and resolved to make the turn off the main road one evening, to see the actual location. Well, one evening, I did more than note the actual spot; I made enquires and received details about service times and other activities. I also started to tune in to the radio programme more regularly on LOVE 101.

I must pause here to say that I wasn't searching for a house of worship as I was already an ardent member of my previous church home holding positions as Chairperson for the Church Council and Coordinator of the Sunday school. However, after a while, I had stopped attending church and so decided to give up these positions. I did so via email on December 4, 2014 at 7:31 in the morning. Taking a break, for me didn't mean leaving that congregation or denomination though. Notwithstanding, I had plateaued. I've always had the desire for continuous spiritual growth and personal development. Therefore, happening upon 'Miracles Now' was nothing shocking. I had been following various religious radio programmes for years. Some favourites include Back to the Bible, which I still enjoy to this date; The

Hour of Decision which is no longer aired; The Lutheran Hour – Bringing Christ to the Nation, Great Christian Hymns of Our Time, Showers of Pentecost and many more, all aired on Radio Jamaica (RJR 94 FM) over the decades. These programmes served to increase my faith and gave me a praise which would sustain me until my next worship day at church.

So back to that left turn to WAFIF that Sunday morning in December 2014; and why I believe it was a move that was ordained by God. (I had completely forgotten the service times given to me the day I had stopped by to make enquiries.) I remember driving onto the church grounds at approximately 7:50 a.m. Were it the usual situation, I would have been 50 minutes late for the first service and 2 hours and 10 minutes early for the second service. It so happened that for this Sunday morning, for whatever reason, only one service was going to be held and that would start at 8 a.m. so I was on time for that. That was a move of God, I believe.

I entered to smiling, warm faces and a pleasant and welcoming ambiance. The Praise and Worship session was a tremendous blessing. One quick observation was the music which was louder than that to which I was accustomed and was a bit distracting for me. However, that was short-lived as I too got caught up with everybody worshipping and just giving praise. It seemed genuine and I sensed that the Spirit of God was indeed in that place. I was happy to be there. Then came the Servant of God who I had been hearing on the radio broadcasts, but now got a chance to see "live and in living colour". He delivered his message with the same fervour, zeal, passion and anointing that define him in the radio programme. Again, there was distraction with the loud monitors and the louder than normal preaching but I concentrated on the message and not the distraction. This style would grow on me. I sensed the Holy Spirit speaking to me clearly, "This is where you should be;" and I responded with a definitive "Yes, this is where I want to be."

To use the cliché, the rest is history. I attended service every Sunday after that. I looked forward to the Word from Bishop Courtney McLean (I now knew his name). I anticipated hearing his voice and when he came forward following praise and worship, I had a good feeling and became expectant for a Word from the true and faithful God who would speak through this servant. I wanted to be connected to this house, WAFIF, and to this Servant of God as led by the Spirit of God who dwells in me.

Soon, I started membership classes and within 7 months I was baptised by immersion on July 5, 2015. Now this was a special moment for more reasons than one; it's a requirement mandated by Jesus Christ and even though I was a Christian and tried to do God's will, I never experienced immersion. In my early years as a Christian, the denomination to which I was connected didn't do immersion. Some years later, when the decision was made to do so, a pool was erected at one of the churches and baptismal services were conducted there. I wanted to experience this spiritual phenomenon since I was "baptised" before the pool was built. I made the request through my church but was later told that the Archbishop would not sanction it because I was already "baptised" and was a good Christian girl anyway so there was no need. I was disappointed and my colleagues at church knew this. I yearned so much to have this wonderful experience.

Baptism within my former denomination, took place during what is called the Easter Vigil service; which is the Saturday after Good Friday; and which was my favourite time on the Christian calendar. We eventually built our own pool at church and during the Easter Vigil service, I would be found in the front pew celebrating with the newly baptised while at the same time wishing I was a part of the immersion experience. Every year during that time, I became reflective, emotional, and teary eyed; and everyone, especially the older members, knew why.

So, July 5, 2015, my immersion day, my new birthday, will remain one of the special moments in my walk with God. I had looked forward to it and I prepared for it. Even writing about it now gives me goose pimples and a happy feeling inside. I also felt it important for the Chief Servant of the house to lead in this experience and so I requested Bishop McLean. I'm glad he accepted because he could have declined the activity to any of his anointed pastors or ministers; and that would have been fine; but I also saw the agreement from the head of the house as an agreement from God.

During the process, before the congregation, when asked all the questions regarding my willingness to take this step; I responded with a resounding "Yes" and "With all my heart." I was bold, I was loud, I was convincing. I let go and placed myself totally in the hands of the brothers who were in the pool with me; and it happened. I was immersed! I came up from the water convinced that Jesus was there with me and He was smiling. As I was led away from the pool I cried for joy. I prayed. I sang in my heart. My heart felt light. I had finally done what was required by God; and I am in this born again experience for the long haul.

My membership classes had started a few weeks after I began attending WAFIF and continued after my baptism. I became a full-fledged member on August 16, 2015. I am now one of the leaders in the Media Department having been placed in charge of the Communications Ministry; and I was also asked to be a Supervisor for Children's Church. I am having fun serving the Lord and I'm experiencing His mighty move in my life through my connection with the Servant of God and to this house of God (WAFIF). I am now following hard after God.

2. The Foundation

I owe a debt of gratitude to St. Peter Claver Church where I had my spiritual foundation. It is Catholic. I was Catholic. It's what I knew. It's how I started my Christian upbringing and my Christian walk. I was practically "born" at St. Peter Claver. I was christened (infant baptism denoted by sprinkling of water on the head) there. I had no interest in any other church or any other denomination. I also am grateful to my god father, Egbert O'Connor, of blessed memory. He was a foundation member and took me to St. Peter Claver for worship. I am thankful to my grandmother, also of blessed memory, who allowed my god father to take me to church.

As I grew, I became involved in all aspects of church life for personal and spiritual development. In the early days, it was Sunday school and Christmas plays. With maturity came participation in retreats and in Cursillos (Wikipedia, 2017) (pronounced ker/see/yos). To explain briefly about the latter; The Cursillo focuses on showing Christian lay people how to become effective Christian leaders over the course of a three-day weekend. We'd go to the venue on Thursday and return home on Sunday. The weekend usually includes fifteen talks, some given by priests and some by lay people. These talks are called "rollos" (pronounced row/yos). The major emphasis of the weekend is to ask participants to take what they have learned back into the world, on what is known as the "fourth day." (This is patterned from the exhortation from Jesus to, "Go into all the world and preach the Good News to everyone;" (Mark 16:15 NLT).

The method stresses personal spiritual development, which is encouraged by weekly group reunions on specific days following the weekend course. Anyone who has been on a Cursillo is known as a Cursillista. So, I'm one such, and the slang for greeting a fellow Cursillista is "De Colores" which means, "in colours". To be "in colours" means to be "in God's grace".

One person for whom I have a lot of respect is former Minister of Tourism, Aloun Assamba, who was formerly Aloun Wood. She was prominent in the Catholic movement and was a popular presenter at retreats. She also featured significantly in my Christian walk as she presented at some of the retreats I attended during those days.

I've had close relationships with many priests and nuns (sisters) who served at St Peter Claver and who have touched my life on my spiritual journey. There were Father Cormac Shanahan, C.P who christened me; Father Sebastian Collupy, a transformational priest, Father Dennis, Father Ramsay, Father Jules Wong who became my best friend for years until he left Jamaica for Rome to study. He never returned having been sent to Canada to serve at a church there. There were also Father Charles Brown, Father Burchel McPherson, who became Bishop of Montego Bay, Father Michael Lewis, Father Thomas, and Father Raphael Assamah. There were many nuns who thought I had the qualities to serve in the convent and who encouraged me to do so. That was not my calling; the leading was not strong in this regard. I bless them all and wish God's continuous blessings upon those who are still alive.

In the Catholic Church, I've done everything; from rushing after primary school was dismissed to clean the rectory (the priests' quarters); to participating in Christmas plays, to teaching Sunday school, to leading the choir, to preparing dramatic scripts for special services, to preparing and doing workshops for lectors (proclaimers of the Word), to making presentations during special seasons on the church's calendar, to rising to the very top of being chairperson of the Parish Advisory Council (church council). I was always asked to serve by the different priests and I did so willingly. I was encouraged to love the Lord and to love my brothers and sisters. Masses (services) were symbolic, rich, and meaningful for those who really loved the Lord and wanted to grow. I participated, experienced, served and reached the peak. Suddenly, I wanted more.

I wanted to take my worship up to the next level. I wanted to move out of the box, to walk on water, to step into the glory realm, to seek the face of God, to hear the voice of God, to fight the principalities and powers! I wanted more! Then I sensed that God was saying, "It's time to move to the next dimension; to take on a new assignment"

The proof of this being a true call from God is the fact that He facilitated the movement that Sunday in December 2014. I've always desired to and tried to surrender to the Lord's direction and leading in my life. The signs were clear and I had no option but to rise to the challenge. I thanked St Peter Claver for the blessing and the part this fine church played in my life; and then I took my leave. I wished Father Assamah the best as they work to build the Kingdom of God with the St. Peter Claver family.

3. Honour–the Simplistic Level

<u>Honouring people is honouring God</u> (WikiHow)

According to Strong's Concordance, "honour" means "renown, glory, splendour."

In my desire to seek more from the Lord; and being a member of WAFIF; Bible study became paramount. I learnt that to receive more, I needed to do more and to give more, including giving honour. The Bible declares that we should honour parents (Ephesians 6:2); the elderly (Leviticus 19:32); and those who lead us (1 Peter 2:17).

This mandate (I'll focus on the latter; honouring those who lead us) from God's inspired Word will be dealt with in more detail in the following chapter. However, I am led to set the pace by highlighting some simple ways to show honour.

<u>Service is vital.</u>

I. Volunteer with an organization or a special charity group. Try to find volunteer work that coincides with your interests. Your place of worship or a charity is a good place to start.

Here are some volunteering options:

- Tutoring or volunteering at a school.
- Coaching a team, if you play a sport

- Cleaning up and working at a park or cultural venue: Emancipation Park, Devon House, Hope Gardens
- Working at a hospital, home for the elderly, children's home, or clinic
- Making calls from home for a fundraising effort

II.   Perform simple good deeds for others casually.

- Yield to a motorist to let him or her merge gradually in traffic
- Prepare a meal for a hungry person who's not a friend or family member
- Hold a door open for someone and smile genuinely when doing so
- Be productive and thoughtful at the workplace
- Be thoughtful of a needy person by providing some clothing or other necessity

Yes, these simple acts show honour to those persons on whom they are performed and, in fact, when we behave in like manner, we are actually honouring God. Don't think they are too simple and that God is bigger than that. For example, how could we associate God with giving a man a 'bligh' in traffic, or holding a door open for someone? It sounds crazy, right? Wrong! We even honour God when we offer sincere condolences in grief; and congratulations in good times. We honour God by giving credit to other people for assistance given, by accepting who and what they are and what they can offer, even though they may be less fortunate than we are. We honour God also by genuinely enjoying time spent with the less fortunate in fellowship. We can change lives through our acts of honour.

We honour God when we show gratitude. Gratitude creates a sense that you have benefited from other people and from things they do and say. When you thank people and accept their importance and share all the hope, peace and other resources that you have, the more you will be able to realize that it is not all about you.

Are you convinced yet? If you don't wish to take MY word for this, how about taking THE Word of God on the subject? *"And when did we see you a stranger, and invite you in, or naked, and clothe you? 'When did we see you sick, or in prison, and come to you?' "The King will answer and say to them, 'Truly I say to you, to the extent that you did it to one of these brothers of Mine, even the least of them, you did it to Me."* (**Matthew 25:38-40 NASB**)

We honour God when we reflect His character to the people around us. God is loving, honest, forgiving, fair, and without sin. When we show others love, speak honestly, forgive those who hurt us, treat others fairly, and ask God's Spirit to help us, we are reflecting God and honouring Him. (Honour God)

4. Honour – The Mandatory Level

An Exhortation From God And His Inspired Word

Let's look at a few Scripture passages focusing on an exhortation to honour. As you reflect on each one; make notes on how it applies to your Man or Woman of God; and how you plan to do daily, what is suggested. Keeping a journal of these activities is a great idea. Please be very honest in your reflection.

Hebrews 13:7 (NLT) - *"Remember your leaders who taught you the Word of God. Think of all the good that has come from their lives, and follow the example of their faith."* **What good has come from your Man/Woman of God? What do you admire most about him/her which you would emulate?**

1Thessalonians 5:12-13 (NLT) - *"Dear brothers and sisters, honour those who are your leaders in the Lord's work. They work hard among you and give you spiritual guidance. Show them great respect and wholehearted love because of their work. And live peacefully with each other."* **What aspect of his/her work do you really admire? How can you show respect and love to him/her**

1 Timothy 2:1-4 (ESV)–*"First of all, then, I urge that supplications, prayers, intercessions, and thanksgivings be made for all people, for kings and all who are in high positions, that we may lead a peaceful and quiet life, godly and dignified in every* *way. This is good, and it is pleasing in the sight of God our Saviour, who desires all people to be saved and to come to the knowledge of the truth."* **Do you pray for and intercede and thank God for your Man/Woman of God daily? Is it a priority for you? Why?**

Romans 13:1 (NLT) – *"Everyone must submit to governing authorities. For all authority comes from God, and all those in positions of authority have been placed there by God."* **What are your thoughts on submission? How do you submit to your Man or Woman of God?**

Galatians 6:6 (NLT) – *"Those who are taught the Word of God should provide for their teachers, sharing all good things with them."* **How much does your Man/Woman of God give priority to the teaching of the Word? How and what do you provide or share with him/her?**

Colossians 3:20 (ESV)–*"Children, obey your parents in everything, for this pleases the Lord."(Message: Remember our pastors are also considered our spiritual parents.)* **How much do you see your pastor as your spiritual parent; especially if he/she is younger than you are?**

2 Chronicles 20:20 (ESV) – *"And they rose early in the morning and went out into the wilderness of Tekoa... Jehoshaphat stood and said, "Hear me, Judah and inhabitants of Jerusalem! Believe in the LORD your God, and you will be established; believe his prophets, and you will succeed."* **How much do you see your Man/Woman of God as a prophet?**

1 Timothy 5:17 (ESV) – *"Let the elders who rule well be considered worthy of double honour, especially those who labour in preaching and teaching.*

The above scripture passages beseech us to honour those whom God has placed in guardianship over us and over our souls. In fact, God's Servants are not just to receive honour but double honour; meaning we respect the office they hold which makes them qualify to be held in high esteem; and, we should go further and honour them in a tangible way. We also are guaranteed success when we do so. Working on the premise that when we honour God's Servant, we are honouring God; God has promised that when I honour Him, He will honour me too; *"...For them that honour me, I will honour, and they that despise me shall be lightly esteemed"***(1 Samuel 2:30 KJV)**. What more could I ask for? This is the more that I want.

It is on this principle therefore that I chose to follow God's Will and receive more by honouring His Chief Servant to whom He has connected me; Bishop Courtney McLean.

This Servant of God is my Shepherd, my Spiritual Father, and based on the Scripture above, the man instituted by God and appointed by God to be in authority over me. I'm therefore expected to be led by him because he's a true Servant of God. If I spiritually reject or resist this Servant of God, I am rejecting or resisting God; and I'm expected to respect and honour him because those virtues are due to him. God gives us choices and I choose to follow hard after God as David did in **Psalm 63:8**. Thus, I believe God has sent me to be connected to His Servant;

and I graciously accept and follow God's lead. Get ready to meet this Man of God; God's Chief Servant.

5. Bishop Courtney McLean

Bishop Courtney McLean is pastor and founder of Worship and Faith International Fellowship- WAFIF; which is one of Jamaica's fastest growing Christian Ministries. It is located in Wedgewood Gardens, at 55 Old Harbour Road; St Catherine. Bishop is an Independent Certified Coach, Teacher and Speaker with The John Maxwell Team. He is a profound preacher, dynamic motivational speaker and philanthropist. He's also the author of two life changing books, "Honouring God- the Gateway to Success" and "Turning Nothing into Something". As stated in the previous chapter, honour is shown to God when we honour the people of God. Bishop McLean has followed the will of God which has equipped him to minister practical and uplifting messages that create positive change and leave individuals across the world empowered.

This Servant of God is married to Reverend Nadine McLean, who is a co-pastor in the ministry; and together they have three beautiful children; two daughters - Deborah, the eldest and Dominique; and a son Daniel.

Living the Vision

The vision of WAFIF is as follows;

Advancing the Kingdom of God through the proclamation of the potent gospel of Jesus Christ; and by the demonstration of the Holy Spirit's power, striving to empower the total man; spirit, soul and body.

Bishop Courtney McLean, by his very life and the activities created with God's leading, has been living up to this vision. The year 2016 was a year in which Bishop McLean undertook a few initiatives to enhance our spiritual growth. A major one was Kingdom Men Connection; where he separated the men from the women and gave these men instructions with a view to teach them and to help them build skills in leadership. The plan was to have them take charge of their families and their marriages where applicable.

The anointed Servant of God, Bishop resolved

(i) to take on the enemy who has been attacking marriages and, with God's help,

(ii) to bring back this noble and sacred institution into alignment.

By so doing, Bishop was actually endorsing and honouring the teachings of Paul as stated in 1 Corinthian 11:3 (NIV): "But I want you to realize that the head of every man is Christ, and the head of the woman is man, and the head of Christ is God"; as well as Ephesians 5:23 (NIV), "For the husband is the head of the wife as Christ is the head of the church, his body, of which he is the Saviour."

The reviews from the men and their wives; as well as the church in general, have been very commendable. Our men are changing for the better and they are learning to lead from the front in their homes. Their change as directed from the leadership of the Servant of God is also a demonstration of their honour of our Bishop, God's Chief Servant.

6. Honour – The Call

My honour of Bishop McLean is demonstrated through my obedience to the call from God. If you truly love the Lord and submit to Him; He will lead you to the House of Worship where He wants you to be connected, like He did to me; and if you continue to be submissive to God; He will lead you to realize why you should and how you may show honour. What is in the Bible will become real to you. My call was manifested in the various situations as revealed in the following pages.

I.   HE'S THE MAN

In the story about David being chosen to be king; God said to Samuel, *"I will reveal to you what you should do: and you will anoint for me the one I point out to you."* **(1 Samuel 16:3 GW)**. So, it was God's choice. Verse 4 says, *"Samuel did what the LORD told him."* Samuel had to obey.

God also confirmed the Servant He placed in authority over me. One night, after a special moment with God; telling Him how much I loved Him and wanted to do His will, I asked fervently how I should go about serving Him; and then retired to bed with the hope that He would answer in His time. I'm not sure if I had started to sleep but what transpired was instructive.

I became aware of being in an unknown place and seeing a man in a grey suit walking ahead of me. The man stopped and turned his body slightly, then turned his head so I could see his face. It was the form of Bishop McLean. His eyes connected with mine as if saying, "Come with me." He then turned again and continued walking and I started to follow. I believe this partnership is God's confirmed plan and I must continue to obey. I MUST HONOUR THIS SERVANT OF GOD.

II.   A WORD

In 2015, I went through a particularly difficult time in my life. A parent from the school that I lead decided to take me to court because, according to her, the insurance fee for her child wasn't paid up. She accused me of embezzlement. This was discovered due to an unfortunate situation which occurred where her daughter lost a piece of her tooth. The parent was right, the money wasn't paid. However, in summarising, when the legal officer came on the parent's behalf, I remembered signing that cheque; which reflected the total amount of insurance paid on behalf of all students, including her daughter, and which should have been paid over to the insurance company. Upon calling my secretary, whose job it was to have the cheques disbursed, I discovered that 6 months later the cheque was still lying in the folder. According to her, she made some calls to the insurance company and didn't get any response and then she forgot. Because of the blessing of God upon my life, I had no fear but expected an amicable resolution. I called the insurance company, spoke to the supervisor who accepted the explanation and graciously decided to accept the cheque. She promised to have someone collect it; of which that was done the very same day. This was a serious matter which could have caused action to be taken against the secretary but I just reprimanded her and left it there.

Having the matter settled and realizing that I was innocent of the charge being laid against me, the bailiff advised the parent to discontinue the suit. However, buoyed by her accomplices, the parent accused me of misappropriating the school's funds generally. She had no proof and the major stakeholder, the Ministry of Education, had never found anything inappropriate with our financial records. The parent also made claims for over half million dollars that she said she lost as a result of travelling to Jamaica to rectify the matter; as well as the money she had spent for dental fees for her child. What she didn't realize and what I also learnt, was that based on the law, it is inappropriate to sue the leader of a school, with regard to matters pertaining to the school. Instead, the case is between the employer (the Ministry of Education) and the complainant (the parent). I had to spend time gathering information and then took documents to the Attorney General's (AG) Chambers. They then collaborated with the Ministry of Education.

A lawyer from the AG's Department was assigned to the case. It saddened me to even think of myself in this sorry state; no one had ever accused me of any misdeed. I enjoyed impeccable reputation and a personality that afforded me the ability to fit comfortably in the company of various types. That parent's and her accomplices' intention, was to erode all this.

The plan of the enemy was to wear away my God given integrity and credibility.

I discussed this matter with Bishop McLean, who prayed for me and promised to be in touch when he received a Word for me. Time went by and I had to be in court for the first mention. It was my very first time dealing with a legal matter, but there was a sense of calm as I knew my God would come through for me. I was very early on the scene and so was the lawyer assigned. The court session began. They called the parent's name but she was absent. The officer went outside to locate her and found her. She came in quite flustered and looking quite nervous. She stated that she did not have a lawyer and asked for time to get same as well as time for the lawyer to gather the necessary information for the case. Her request was granted and a new date for one month later was set for the hearing. I said or was asked nothing. The lawyer spoke on my behalf. In the meantime, I reported what transpired to Bishop and he told me to continue praying as he was doing same and that he still had not yet received a specific Word for me.

About a fortnight after the hearing, a document was delivered to my office. It stated that the parent had decreased her demand of over half million dollars in medical expenses and other bills to a very small amount comparatively. The Lord was on the case and prayers of the Bishop as well as my prayers were working.

One week before the next hearing, I was at the 7o'clock Sunday service as usual. It was a special service; there was an anointing and the Holy Spirit reigned supreme. Bishop was led to lay hands on the members. He told us to pray earnestly as he went through the aisles laying hands on each member. I was deep in prayer, not realizing that he had reached my row. As he touched me he whispered in my ear, "**Psalm 35.**" He got the Word for me! I received and accepted it gladly and with thanksgiving.

For that entire week, I worked the Word; morning, evening and sometimes during the day at school. I also distinctly remembered praying for that parent asking the Lord to forgive her as she didn't realize what she was doing and was just being used by another power which wasn't of God. I remembered feeling a peace in my heart for her. During that week also, I received a call from the lawyer and she told me that I didn't need to be at the hearing as she would represent the Ministry of Education. She promised to give me a feedback. The Word was working already as I considered that good news.

The day of the hearing came; and I again prayed the Word given by the Servant of God and waited to hear what transpired. By midday, I got a call from the lawyer who stated that the parent didn't show up and that the judge had dismissed the case. The Word from God through His servant worked!

I MUST HONOUR THIS SERVANT OF GOD.

III.   THE TOUCH

There was a period in 2015 when I experienced severe financial constraints. My salary was very low because I was servicing a loan taken to finance my daughter's education. I therefore became dependent on the travel allowance paid to school leaders by the Ministry of Education. This money was due to be paid monthly but sometimes there were financial challenges at the Ministry of Education; and there were delays in payment.

During that difficult period, lasting about three months when there was a delay in receiving this allowance. I prayed and I kept checking my account repeatedly but no funds were available. It got bad. All financial options were blocked and I really didn't have any money. I got tired of checking my account to see if funds were uploaded. After being disappointed repeatedly, I decided to take a break from checking for another month. During all this time however, I never stopped worshipping the Lord and believing Him for a breakthrough.

I went to my house of worship. It was one of those Sundays when Bishop McLean walked the aisles and pews and blessed persons as he was led by the Holy Spirit. I held my head down in fervent prayer and my hands were raised as I prayed. Soon after, I felt a hand in mine. It was Bishop's. The feeling that I experienced when he touched me was one of calm assurance; as if to say, "All is well, your breakthrough is here; rest." I had not discussed this with Bishop, but with the special anointing upon his life, I believe he sensed my situation and was led by God to assure me. Immediately after service, I rushed to the ATM and my expectations were realized. My travel allowance had come.

I MUST HONOUR THIS SERVANT OF GOD

IV.   JUST DO IT

For years, I've been struggling with the demon of procrastination. This has caused me to lose out on so many opportunities which in turn have caused me to lose out on additional income, useful networking, better health, meeting deadlines, adding value to people's lives, making an impact and professional enhancement.

I've had a portfolio for the National College of Educational Leadership (NCEL) which was due in May 2016. This is toward completion of part 2 of my Effective Principals Certification. Up until November 2016, it still had not been submitted; and the main reason was procrastination. Then there is also my manuscript written for the Grade 6 exit Common Entrance exam, mentioned earlier, which I've had for decades just lying on my bookshelf; unpublished.

In comes the inspiration from the Servant of God, Bishop Courtney McLean, who hosts 'Born to Win' Conferences, preaches sermons and produces 'Facebook Live' presentations; which all serve to encourage his patrons, congregations and visitors. He tells us that there is greatness in us; that we are of value, and that we are to find our prophetic destiny; and with God's help, to step into this destiny. He says, "JUST DO IT –DON'T DELAY!"

World famous author, John Maxwell has made some valuable pronouncements which bear repeating. He said, "Most people wake up in the mornings waiting for someone to make their day." He discourages this. He believes people are to be intentional and make the connection with people that will add value to their lives. John Maxwell states that, "The great connectors always give a lot of energy." My Servant of God epitomizes what John Maxwell says. Bishop McLean says, 'Jump out of bed, not roll out'; 'Rise before the World'; 'Don't neutralize your mobility.' In his 'Facebook Live' presentations, he begins with a resounding "Good morning, good morning, good morning" between 5 and 6 o'clock; and he is full of energy and ready to connect. At that time of day, you would appreciate and understand that many people are still in bed; and some are probably not in the mood initially; but for those who are, it is clear that Bishop loves his people; has their interest at heart and genuinely enjoys pushing us to the next level of our potential. The general feeling is that Bishop does not focus on himself, but instead on the people with whom he connects.

I have always known that I am special and that I can "do it" whatever "it" is. However, Bishop has taken the "born to win;" "wired to win" and "you have greatness within you" initiatives to another level; so much so, that the hearer wants to make the effort and in fact does. I am pleased to report that my portfolio was submitted during the first week of December 2016. Also, my manuscript was taken off the shelf with the intention of doing the necessary tweaking to satisfy the current situation; and then I will be doing the research to get publishing advice.

I am also planning to do a compilation of my Facebook devotions with the intention to publish. You are also reading this book which came out of this new-found energy and aspiration and realization of my full potential. God has given each of us one talent or more and we simply need to press into Him to discover the plan He has for us. We need to honour God by using this plan to glorify Him and to add value to the lives of others. Bishop McLean has facilitated this by believing in me.

I MUST HONOUR THIS SERVANT OF GOD.

V.   EVERYTHING I HAVE......

I will briefly mention that at another of our services of laying on of hands, Bishop McLean, when he got to me, whispered, "Everything I have, I give to you.' That was big for me. I interpreted that to mean, his anointing, his spirit, his energy, his success, his prosperity, his fivefold ministry....as he said...EVERYTHING.

In addition to that, I believe he was saying, "Just do all you have to do, don't procrastinate; use my zeal to give you the energy you need." This is big stuff.

I MUST HONOUR THIS SERVANT OF GOD.

VI.   YOU'RE CALLED

One Saturday night during my devotion at home, I told God of my desire to delve deeper into Him; following which I retired to bed. I woke the following morning with a revelation of how I should deepen my spiritual life. I kept this close to my heart as Mary the Mother of Jesus did when the shepherds declared the wonders about her Son at His birth **(Luke 2:17-19)**.

I got ready and went to church. I declared it a day of thanksgiving as I knew the Lord had spoken to me. The praise and worship segment was a tremendous blessing. It was as if all in the sanctuary were of one mind, heart, soul and spirit.

The Man of God then came to bring the Word. Lo and behold, what was my revelation became the topic of Bishop McLean's sermon. I saw it as an endorsement and was very excited to share this with him at the end of the service. Following the service, I waited my turn as there usually is a line of persons who wish to engage the Bishop. Then it was my turn. I was received graciously as usual; which is a characteristic of this Servant of God. He makes you feel welcomed, he treats you with respect; and when you are in his presence, you recognize that you're in the presence of an anointed Servant of God.

I told him about my prayer the night before, my revelation the following morning, the fact that it formed the topic of his sermon; and that I saw it as an endorsement. The Servant of God smiled and said to me, "You're called, just know that you're called Woman of God." Again, I kept this and pondered it in my heart.

Some months later, on December 17, 2016, in preparing the content for my daily devotion posted on Facebook; the Scripture of the Day was **Psalm 119:10 (KJV)**- "*With my whole heart have I sought thee: O let me not wander from thy commandments.*" I equated this to **Psalm 63:8**, where David said his soul followed hard after God. I encouraged my readers to do like David and follow hard after God. I told them to stay in His Word so they will remain steadfast in their pursuit and in doing

God's will. However, in studying the Bible and in doing the research, I was convinced about something wonderful which Bishop had told me months before; which is that I am already called. The fact that I have the desire to know more about God; as well as the desire to please Him, means that He already had a desire for me and pursued me. Here's the proof; "No man can come to me, except the Father which hath sent me draw him." (John 6:44 KJV). That blew me away! It is now my turn to continue the pursuit. The Man of God saw this and revealed it to me.

I MUST HONOUR THIS SERVANT OF GOD.

7. Honour – The Benefits

Honour is sanctioned and supported by God. There are numerous benefits to honouring those set in authority over us for our spiritual growth. Therefore, when I honour God's Chief Servant, as Bishop Courtney McLean is, I expect great remuneration; because God says so. He is not known to lie; it is not His character to lie. His Word is truth **(John 17:17 NIV)**. Two of my favourite scriptures are set out below. The first shows how God honours me directly;

1 Samuel 2:30 (ASV) – *"Therefore Jehovah, the God of Israel, saith, I said indeed that thy house, and the house of thy father, should walk before me forever: but now Jehovah saith, Be it far from me; for them that honour me I will honour, and they that despise me shall be lightly esteemed."*

Likewise, when I honour God's Chief Servant, God also honours me:

Matthew 10:41 (NLT) – *"If you receive a prophet as one who speaks for God, you will be given the same reward as a prophet. And if you receive righteous people because of their righteousness, you will be given a reward like theirs."* When I reflect on this Word from God, I become extremely humbled by the word spoken to me by my Bishop, "Everything I have I give to you."

As mentioned in Chapter 3; and using Strong's Concordance's definition, "honour" means "renown, glory, splendour."

Wouldn't you want to honour God by honouring the Servant of God and then be clothed in the beauty, glory and splendour of His Majesty? I believe you would.

8. Honour – Consequences of the Lack Thereof

Just as there are benefits to honouring God through honouring the Servant of God; there could be painful or tragic results if there is no honour: Here are a few Scripture passages to prove.

I. CONVERSATION BETWEEN JEHOVAH AND SAMUEL (VASU, 2007)

1 Samuel 2:30, although used in the previous section to demonstrate the benefit of honouring God, is also quite appropriate in showing the result of dishonouring. It serves a two-fold purpose. I believe the Amplified Version (AMP) of this Scripture sums it up very well; *"Therefore the LORD God of Israel declares, 'I did indeed say that your house and that of [Aaron] your father would walk [in priestly service] before Me forever.' But now the LORD declares, 'Far be it from Me—for those who honour Me I will honour, and those who despise Me will be insignificant and contemptible.*

I can't imagine what would happen to me or how I would feel if my heavenly Father should degrade me or hold me contemptible or see me as insignificant.

II.   THE STORY OF DAVID AND SAUL (VASU, 2007)

2 Samuel 1:1-16 (AMP) – *"Now it happened after the death of Saul, when David had returned from the slaughter of the Amalekites, that he stayed two days in Ziklag. On the third day a man came [unexpectedly] from Saul's camp with his clothes torn and dust on his head [as in mourning]. When he came to David, he bowed to the ground and lay himself face down [in an act of great respect and submission]. Then David asked him, "Where do you come from?" He said, "I have escaped from the camp of Israel." David said to him, "How did it go? Please tell me." He answered, "The people have fled from the battle. Also, many of the people have fallen and are dead; Saul and Jonathan his son are also dead." So David said to the young man who informed him, "How do you know Saul and his son Jonathan are dead?" And the young man who told him explained, "By chance I happened to be on Mount Gilboa, and there was Saul leaning on his spear, and the chariots and horsemen [of the Philistines] were close behind him. When he turned to look behind him, he saw me, and called to me. And I answered, 'Here I am.' He asked me, 'Who are you?' I answered him, 'I am an Amalekite.' He said to me, 'Stand up facing me and kill me, for [terrible] agony has come over me, yet I still live [and I will be taken alive].' So I stood facing him and killed him, because I knew that he could not live after he had fallen. Then I took the crown which was on his head and the band which was on his arm, and I have brought them here to my lord."*

Then David grasped his own clothes and tore them [in mourning]; so did all the men who were with him. They mourned and wept and fasted until evening for Saul and Jonathan his son, and for the LORD'S people and the house of Israel, because they had fallen by the sword [in battle]. David said to the young man who informed him, "Where are you from?" He answered, "I am the son of a foreigner (resident alien, sojourner), an Amalekite." David said to him, "How is it that you were not afraid to put out your hand to destroy the LORD'S anointed?" David called one of the young men and said, "Go, execute him." So he struck the Amalekite and he died. David said to the [fallen] man, "Your blood is on your own head, for your own mouth has testified against you, saying, 'I have killed the LORD'S anointed.'"

The message here is straightforward: No matter what you think of the Man of God, or what he has done, he must be honoured as he was anointed by God. Leave the judgement to God.

III.   ELISHA AND THE YOUNG BOYS (VASU, 2007)

2 Kings 2:23-24 (AMP) – *"Then Elisha went up from Jericho to Bethel. On the way, young boys came out of the city and mocked him and said to him, "Go up, you baldhead! Go up, you baldhead!" When he turned around and looked at them, he cursed them in the name of the LORD. Then two female bears came out of the woods and tore to pieces forty-two of the boys."*

Message: Never mock God's anointed; death might be your portion. The mockers were young boys. This is usually considered normal being the usual mischief in which boys get involved. However, age is no factor when it comes to being cursed by God for dishonour to His servant.

IV.   THE DECEPTION BY NOAH'S SON(VASU, 2007)

Genesis 9: 20-27 (AMP) – *"And Noah began to farm and cultivate the ground and he planted a vineyard. He drank some of the wine and became drunk, and he was uncovered and lay exposed inside his tent. Ham, the father of Canaan, saw [by accident] the nakedness of his father, and [to his father's shame] told his two brothers outside. So Shem and Japheth took a robe and put it on both their shoulders, and walked backwards and covered the nakedness of their father; their faces were turned away so that they did not see their father's nakedness. When Noah awoke from his wine [induced stupor], he knew what his younger son [Ham] had done to him. So he said, "Cursed be Canaan [the son of Ham]; A servant of servants. He also said, "Blessed be The LORD, the God of Shem; and let Canaan be his servant. "May God enlarge [the land of] Japheth and let him dwell in the tents of Shem; and let Canaan be his servant."*

Message: Never humiliate God's anointed; you'll be cursed. There wasn't only a curse pronounced on the villain; but blessings were bestowed on those who were considerate and showed honour.

V.   JESUS AND THE DIGNITARIES FROM
JERUSALEM(VASU, 2007)

Mark 3:22-30 (AMP) – *"The scribes who came down from Jerusalem were saying, "He is possessed by Beelzebul (Satan)," and "He is driving out the demons by the [power of the] ruler of the demons." So He called them to Himself and spoke to them in* parables, "How can Satan drive out Satan? If a kingdom is divided [split into factions and rebelling] against itself, that kingdom cannot stand. And if a house is divided against itself, that house cannot stand. And if Satan has risen up against himself and is divided, he cannot stand, but is coming to an end. But no one can go into a strong man's house and steal his property unless he first overpowers and ties up the strong man, and then he will ransack and rob his house. I assure you and most solemnly say to you, all sins will be forgiven the sons of men, and all the abusive and blasphemous things they say; but whoever blasphemes against the Holy Spirit and His power [by attributing the miracles done by Me to Satan] never has forgiveness, but is guilty of an everlasting sin [a sin which is unforgivable in this present age as well as in the age to come]"— Jesus said this] because the scribes and Pharisees were [attributing His miracles to Satan by] saying, "He has an unclean spirit."

Message: When miracles are done through the Servant of God and there's doubt; it could be detrimental to your soul. The sin of blasphemy will not be forgiven.

VI.   **JESUS AND THE FAMILIAR NEIGHBOURS** (VASU, 2007)

Mark 6:1-6 (AMP) – *"Jesus left there and came to His hometown [Nazareth]; and His disciples followed Him. When the Sabbath came, He began to teach in the synagogue; and many who listened to Him were astonished, saying, "Where did this man get these things [this knowledge and spiritual insight]? What is this wisdom [this confident understanding of the Scripture] that* *has been given to Him, and such miracles as these performed by His hands? Is this not the carpenter, the son of Mary, and the brother of James and Joses and Judas and Simon? Are His sisters not here with us?" And they were [deeply] offended by Him [and their disapproval blinded them to the fact that He was anointed by God as the Messiah]. Jesus said to them, "A prophet is not without honour (respect) except in his hometown and among his relatives and in his own household." And He could not do a miracle there at all [because of their unbelief] except that He laid His hands on a few sick people and healed them. He wondered at their unbelief.*

And He was going around in the villages teaching."

Message: Don't become too familiar with the Man or Woman of God; you could lose out on your blessings. The people of His hometown could not see it in themselves to accept that Jesus, with whom they were familiar, had the wisdom and power to teach with such authority; and to do all the supernatural things they saw and heard. Their dishonour "cramped" Jesus' style and He <u>could not</u> perform any miracles. The same Jesus with whom nothing was impossible found it impossible to do great miracles. Dishonour brought out a disability in Jesus.

9. Honour - From the Pen of an Authority (Part 1)

It is deliberate that I decided to include this chapter about honouring God's Chief Servant. Bishop McLean has been fighting hard for the institution of marriage as he holds it in high esteem. He preaches about marriage; he holds presentations with marriage as the theme; and most commendable of all, he leads by example. His marriage is seen as one to emulate; and he readily yields to vulnerability which is attractive to his hearers, especially the men. They recognize that he has not always enjoyed the success that his marriage currently has; and that he's had to work hard at it. When a servant of God opens his life to the members of his congregation; and becomes real with them, he gains their trust and support. The members in turn receive the desire to also take the journey for success in their marriages. Testimonials of how Bishop McLean has assisted in repairing broken marriages are commendable; and provide further support for the reasons this Servant of God should be honoured.

Notwithstanding however, the great effort being made to get our men to become Kingdom men; as well as to get their counterparts to be supportive; is matched with the similar or greater effort by the enemy to thwart, block, break, damage, dismantle, disintegrate the plans of God. All believers are aware that where there is evidence of success in God's family, the enemy pushes harder; to tear down that family structure. For those who are married, he attacks marriages, taking God's original plan for the family out of alignment.

With the foregoing, I therefore thought of including this section, bringing into awareness how ruthless the enemy is at his game; and how, through the wiles of demonic forces, the effort of God's Chief Servant, may become eroded. In this chapter, you see how, through a lack of knowledge and understanding, the demon can cause one party or both parties in a union of marriage, to go down a very destructive pathway where souls are sold and lost forever, unless there is Divine intervention.

Every day as I grow in my Christian walk, I've come to realize that gaining knowledge is such an intrinsic part of building Kingdom people. No wonder Bishop McLean implores us ever so often to pray, push, fast, sow seeds and stay in the glory realm. He encourages us to engage in Bible study; make notes of and invest in CD's on sermons; and read books to enhance our personal, professional and Spiritual life. He insists that we never stop climbing as we aspire to get to the next dimension in our Christian life. A lack of knowledge has caused believers to engage in some soul killing, spirit chasing, body wrecking activities that they think are normal. What they don't realize is that there is nothing normal about something that has the capacity to drive you out of your mind; to cause you to fail in health and wealth; and to take you to the pits of hell; sometimes with no hope of returning.

In this section, I have been led by God to show how the enemy may attack a marriage. It is being done with the intention that you, the reader, will use the knowledge to assist you to veer from the path taken by the character in the story, and which almost brought a tragic end to his marriage. This will be shared through a blog, written in September 2013 and is entitled, 'The Dangers of Dishonour.' (The Danger of Dishonour, 2013) It was written by Mike Phillips (a brief profile is showed in Appendix 1) and is one of two articles which I will share from Mark from his blog platform 'The Gates Are Open. 'Here's the first story verbatim.

I.   THE DANGER OF DISHONOUR(THE DANGER OF DISHONOUR, 2013)

September 23, 2013

Stuart and I prayed for a half hour about his wife. She was suffering through a series of painful attacks, bizarre maladies that seemed unrelated to each other. Her doctors could not find the cause. She had migraine headaches, chest pain, nausea, joint irritation, ear infection, low fevers, foot pain, tremors and panic attacks.

During the previous six months, she had seen a gynaecologist, neurologist, arthritic specialist, gastroenterologist, pain specialist, physiotherapist and immunologist, and was now being sent to both a psychologist and psychiatrist. Having failed to find any physical cause which would tie in all of these symptoms, the doctors decided they needed to check if her emotional state caused all of these problems. This referral to the psychiatrist seemed to mock her pain, and she gave up trying to fight it all.

As I was praying, I had a thought that this may not have a physical root cause. I sensed an enemy of the soul, an unclean spirit, was attacking her. Though I have not seen this happen often, I know it does occur. But because this is not a common reason for people being ill, I kept quiet about it. I continued asking the Holy Spirit for more insight into this, and as I did, another thought went through my mind. I acted on it.

"Stuart, do you have a problem with pornography?"

"Sometimes. I don't like to admit it, but I view porn every couple of weeks."

"Just porn? Have you ever acted on your fantasies with other women?"

He hesitated and looked down. This, coupled with his worried expression, lent me courage to press further.

"What have you done, Stu?" He then began telling me about a web site he had joined several months earlier which allowed married people to find sexual partners with other married people.

After telling me about a number of women he had talked to, he assured me he had never met any of them in person. He was quite adamant that he did this because of curiosity, not because he wanted an affair. I had heard variations of his story from a lot of men and women.

I knew my next question was most critical. His answer may hold the key to his wife's illness. "Stu, did you talk about your wife with any of the women?" He blanched openly at my question.

"A lot of the women wanted to know why I was on the web site. It bothered me that they asked what was so wrong with my marriage that would lead me to seek out an affair. So I told them some stories. I have to admit Mike that many of the things I said weren't true. I lied to a few women."

"What did you tell them?"

"I told them all that my wife didn't want sex any more, that she was only interested in the kids and her business. Which, of course, is not true at all."

What I told him next is the basis of this article. Stuart had dishonoured his wife. To honour someone means to show respect to them, to show how they are important and special in our lives and in general. Therefore, to dishonour a person means to disrespect them, lie about them or act like they are unimportant. I explained to Stuart how his dishonour had started with his porn usage. By looking at hundreds of women in various sexual poses and situations, he had downgraded his wife to lesser status. This made it so much easier for him to lie to other women and tell them how unimportant his wife was to him. I explained this was only the beginning of his problems.

After a while, he stopped me and asked "So, what you're saying is that my wife's illnesses are God's judgment on her for the way I've acted?"

"Stu, that's not it at all. God forgave all your sins on the cross. He has washed you clean by the blood of Jesus. You are not guilty in God's eyes. The Bible says "There is therefore now no condemnation for those who are in Christ Jesus." No, it is not God who is bringing these illnesses upon your wife. God himself does not bring disaster and illness upon us. God is love and would never harm us. But there is a class of beings in this universe whose sole purpose is to steal, kill and destroy our lives (John 10:10). Collectively, we call these beings "Satan", but they really are a host of opportunistic spirits looking to attack and destroy our lives. However, they are not allowed to attack us unless they have permission."

"How do they get permission?"

"If people commit certain sins over a period of time, then the enemy is allowed to attack in those areas." I explained to Stuart some of the verses from the Bible which show this, and then came back to my explanation of events.

"Stuart, your relationship with your wife is a covenant relationship. In spiritual terms, the covenant is the deepest promise you can make to a person. You may not know it, but to do harm to that covenant is to do harm to yourself and to her. Satan's name means "accuser". He loves to act as the Prosecuting attorney before God, claiming that we are guilty of crimes and need to be punished. When those crimes are against God, he will not allow us to be attacked. But when the crimes involve others, especially when we hurt those closest to us, we incur the wrath of the Accuser. You have dishonoured your wife. There are few ways you could have acted worse than this."

Here is the end of his story: He repented before God for his actions, quit the website and stopped viewing porn (this last part took a longer time to correct, but that's another blog entry). He then anointed his wife with oil and we prayed for her.

From that day, her symptoms stopped and have not recurred.

I believe there are four keys to overcoming dishonour.

1.   Repent. This means more than just saying you're sorry to God. It means to acknowledge and understand what you're doing wrong and choose actions that counter-act it. Breaking off bad relationships, apologizing for hurts, cutting off access to things or people that make it worse – all of these are repentant actions.

2.   Change: Get to the roots of why you do what you do. A counsellor or coach can help with this.

3.   Accountability: Admit to others what you have done and ask them to watch for it from you and call you on it if you persist in doing it.

4.   Pray for Blessing. The Bible tells us we are to bless others and not curse them. If we have cursed our spouse through dishonour, dedicate the future to blessing them through word, deed and prayer. **(Reprinted with permission)**

(End of the article)

I found this article real, educational, informative and enlightening. As I read I couldn't help but make notes of my take away points which will serve me well personally but which have provided a knowledge base for relevant and suitable content for sharing.

Here are some points that I garnered from the article. I invite you to also note your takeaway points so that we can be 'armed and dangerous' in the event of an enemy attack, bearing in mind that we are on the battleground; as the writer says in the article, "...there is a class of beings in this universe whose sole purpose is to steal, kill and destroy our lives (John 10:10).

I've noted that:

- In times when the 'ruler of this dark earth' has taken over, only someone who is experienced and knowledgeable in the Spirit realm can provide the deliverance. Mike had the experience and was knowledgeable. He was therefore able to work with the villain to provide the release and bring about a solution. Bishop McLean heads a well structured and organized team comprising intercessors, a Deliverance Minister and other Ministers under the five-fold ministry. He instituted First Fruit Fridays under the direction of the Holy Spirit, where every first Friday the members engage in "all night until daylight" prayers and "war" to tear down strongholds and to come into our prophetic destiny.

- The enemy is beaten with the Word; nothing beats the power of prayer when the enemy attacks. Mike obviously believed in the power of prayer. It was his prayers with Stu that formed the basis for the healing. On Tuesdays at WAFIF, our Chief Servant of God engages us in Bible study where we focus on the Word and are taught to use the Word to receive our breakthrough. One particularly enlightening series of our Bible Study sessions was 'Repentance from Dead Works.' The highlight of this series was the virtue of repentance which is intrinsic for a changed life; a point which was also very significant in the story of dishonour told earlier. Repentance is one of the keys to overcoming dishonour.

- Under severe enemy attack, it's not just a one-shot prayer but continuous and consistent prayers that will bring healing and permanent results. Mike got a revelation about the problem; but he wanted confirmation; so he continued to press into the Holy Spirit and got his answer. As I reflect on this point; it is not unusual during our regular Sunday services or all night prayer services to hear our Servant of God saying, "Come on church, Pray! Pray! Pray!" He pushes you, drives you and leads you to pray without ceasing. After a while, it becomes easy. He is just a mighty and anointed Servant of God who is always pushing his sheep to climb higher in the Lord.

- Being human, if there's no proper spiritual foundation, the usual option under severe enemy attack is to give up. Stuart's wife quit fighting after repeatedly taking medications and visiting numerous specialists and receiving no relief. Bishop McLean teaches us never to give up; as a matter of fact, his regular expression is, "push!"

- The great breakthrough called the 'Internet' or 'Social Media' which has reduced the world to a mere global village, has proven to be a hindrance; and actually provides a "window" for the entrance of the enemy. The enemy's attack on Stuart's wife came as a result of him gaining an interest in and feeding that interest from a porn website. Our Chief Servant uses this potential hindrance of Social Media as a breakthrough media, via "Facebook", our website –"wafifglory.com;" and Instagram. His "Facebook Live" presentations became a staple, teaching and encouraging members and visitors alike and assuring us of our greatness, of God's love for us and the fact that we were 'Born to Win' and 'Wired to Win'. His '73-Days' journey on Facebook at 5 o'clock every morning in early 2017 is still a reference point to this day. In fact, it gave rise to a huge Conference attended by over 250 patrons at Knutsford Court Hotel. At that Conference intimate stories were shared, new relationships were started and tears flowed naturally. It was a beautiful, blessed, spiritual experience; all led by God's Chief Servant, Bishop Courtney McLean and supported by the able Courtney McLean Team.

- When the enemy enters and causes dishonour in a marriage, it doesn't necessarily start through physical sexual contact; Stu claimed that he had no physical contact with any of the ladies from the porn site. Usually the basis for the sin facilitates the compounding of the sin. He never made physical contact but in order to feed his fantasies and stay active, Stu had to declare some stuff which proved him to be a liar and a deceiver, which intensified the situation. Our Bishop constantly implores us to steer clear of doing things to grieve the Holy Spirit. One of the core values of WAFIF is "love". This Servant of God reminds us through this core value that *"love covers a multitude of sins"***(1 Peter 4:8)** including lying and deceiving as were evident in the story with Stu and Mike

- We give the enemy permission to attack when we constantly (operative word) sin in a particular area. For example, spreading rumours against people, threatening, deceiving or being abusive to someone as well as neglecting the vulnerable among us, open a window for the enemy. It is important for us to constantly protect ourselves with *"the full armour of God, so that when the day of evil comes, you may be able to stand your ground, and after you have done everything, to stand. Stand firm then, with the belt of truth buckled around your waist, with the breastplate of righteousness in place, and with your feet fitted with the readiness that comes from the gospel of peace. In addition to all this, take up the shield of faith, with which you can extinguish all the flaming arrows of the evil one. Take the helmet of salvation and the sword of the Spirit, which is the word of God. And pray in the Spirit on all occasions with all kinds of prayers and requests. With this in mind, be alert and always keep on praying for all the Lord's people."***(Ephesians 6:13-18 NIV)**. If not, we fall easy prey to the wiles of the devil; so *"Stay alert! Watch* *out for your great enemy, the devil. He prowls around like a roaring lion, looking for someone to devour."* **(1 Peter 5:8 NLT).** Our Servant of God constantly states and also advises his congregation not to be perturbed about what people want to say in spreading bad news or rumours or gossip. He implores persons rather, to ask him about himself as he is better able to tell about himself than anyone else can; which usually elicits laughter but the message is solid nonetheless.

- To get deliverance one must repent of the act which causes the enemy to enter; and then quit the action. Stu repented, quit viewing the website and prayed for the possessed – his wife.

I tried to highlight the worth of Bishop McLean with each of the takeaway points stated earlier. I must thank this Servant of God. The importance of knowledge in fighting the attacks of the enemy was mentioned earlier. If Mike was not knowledgeable and discerning, he would not have been able to have the inclination of what possibly could be the problem. I must also acknowledge again, my Bishop's effort. With God's leading on his life; he has led us into "Repentance from Dead Works" at Bible Study; and has been teaching our men how to become Kingdom men who must take charge of their lives by becoming the excellent leaders God ordained them to be in their families, their marriages and in the church. Bishop must also be commended for leading the charge by demonstrating with his own life. I MUST HONOUR THIS SERVANT OF GOD

What points have you garnered from reading the article? Write your reflections here:

....

....

....

....

....

....

....

....

....

....

....

....

....

....

....

....

10. Honour - From the Pen of an Authority (Part 2)

Welcome to Part 2 of the promised article by counsellor and writer, Mike Phillips. In Part 1, the article shared, focused on how the enemy sets out to steal, kill and destroy relationships; especially marriage. What it did was show how an act of dishonour may be manifested and the extent to which it may impact the lives of those close to you.

In this article, the concept of honour is featured for what it is; and it demonstrates one fact; that we need to show honour. It is shared as a part of a series entitled 'Ten Healthy Ideas' where the author encouraged his readers to have a healthy outlook for the New Year (2014). He shared an idea each day for ten days. The piece on honour was shared on Day 3. In this article also, the author makes reference to his previous article (Part 1), that was shared in the previous chapter. The decision to include this piece is because both articles complement each other. I hope you find it useful as I did. Here it is verbatim:

Honour to Whom Honour is Due

December 22, 2013

In the 1924 Olympics, U.S. sprinter Jackson Schultz sent a note to British runner Eric Liddell. Both of them were Christians, and Liddell had refused to run on a Sunday because it violated his beliefs that Sunday should be a day set apart for God. (In the movie, Liddell is seen as finding out about his heat being run on the Sunday as he gets on the boat. In reality, he found out months before and pulled out of the competition before being chosen. But his stance was known throughout the world.)

In his note, sent weeks before the Olympics, Schultz told Liddell how he admired him for standing up for what he believed. Schultz also believed this stance would be the deciding factor whether Liddell won his race–the 400 meters. At the end of his letter, he wrote: "As the Good Book says, "He who honours Me, him will I honour." History records that Liddell did win the 400 meters and beat one of Schultz's close friends to set the Olympic record.

But was Schultz right? In the note he sends Liddell, he quotes 1 Samuel 2:30, which says:

"Therefore the Lord, the God of Israel, declares: 'I promised that members of your family would minister before me forever.' But now the Lord declares: 'Far be it from me! Those who honour me I will honour, but those who despise me will be disdained."

Schultz apparently believed that if someone takes a stand for God, in the end, God will honour that person. I'm not sure I totally agree. Many who have stood for God have seen their dreams shattered and been made fools of by this world. But I also believe that those who do what God commands will make more out of their lives than those who dishonour God.

I think there is a principle here that would certainly do us well to remember. Our relationship with God is a covenant. It requires both parties to maintain an honourable place in order for all the benefits of the relationship to be experienced.

A covenant relationship is one that is supposed to last for the rest of one's life. There are very few of these because of that. A parent and child, husband and wife, certain lifelong friendships, God and a believer and fellow members of God's church are examples of true covenant relationships. One of the great benefits of those relationships is the concept of honour.

The word honour means to show respect to someone, to show how they are important and special in our lives. I believe there are spiritual things which happen when we honour another person. We strengthen the bindings between us and them and we allow for spiritual blessings to come to both parties. But, of course, the same is also true for dishonour. When we dishonour someone with whom we share a deep covenant relationship, we weaken the ties between us and allow spiritual destruction in our lives. I explore this concept in marriage in an earlier article.

The Bible tells children to "honour their parents". Husbands and wives are supposed to show honour to their spouses. Friends are to honour deep friendship by telling the truth, giving aid when needed, coming to the rescue, keeping confidence and not betraying one another.

In the case of children, we are told it is the first commandment with a promise:

Eph. 6:2-3: "Honour your father and mother"—which is the first commandment with a promise, so that it may go well with you and that you may enjoy long life on the earth."

Honouring our parents releases health and life blessings upon us and them.

Jim suffered from multiple ailments all the time. He had over 40 pills he took each day for one problem or another. As he and I worked together in counselling over a year, our goal was to eliminate most of those medications. During therapy, we identified a number of false beliefs he carried with him and other detrimental elements related to un-forgiveness. At one point, he had eliminated a good *portion of his drugs. That's when we came to the hardest part of the counselling journey.*

"Mike, I want nothing to do with my kids. They are all whiners and they never do anything but bring me grief. I can't really stand to be around any of them." I explained to Jim that it was proper to have boundaries so others cannot hurt us. But I also asked Jim if he had ever blessed his children. He had really never spoken blessings over any of them. Had he praised them? He said they had never done anything worth praising. Had he told others how much he appreciated any of them? Had he bragged about them? On the contrary, he often criticized them to anyone who listened.

I explained to him why honour is important. God sets the example for this. Even though we have all treated God poorly, God never gives up on us. He never stops loving us. And God will never curse us. God will warn us and discipline us as children, but he always wants blessings for our lives. But when we refuse to honour those who are in covenant relationships with us, we allow the enemy of our souls to attack us and defeat us. Our bodies, minds, emotions and life goals are often destroyed. Those who are critical and dishonouring of their loved ones will often pay the price in personal destruction.

Jim decided to begin blessing those around him. He stopped putting down his children and wife to other people. He asked God regularly to bless them. He sent them notes encouraging them and telling them why he was proud of each one. He began to keep a journal and wrote down why he appreciated his wife and each of his kids.

Six months later, he didn't need any more medications. He has seen a remarkable change in his life since then. As he has honoured the people in his life, the effects of dishonour are being eliminated.

This works with people at church, our relatives and friends and our spouses. We may not like all they do, and we cannot endorse wicked and misguided schemes. But we can honour them and their relationship to us even if we have to maintain a few boundaries.

*If you do that, you will see health come to you and them.(**Reprinted with permission**)*

(End of article)

Like the article in the previous chapter, this also left me with food for thought. The section highlighting Jim and his behaviour towards his children and the subsequent occurrence was a big take-away point for me. I will use my daughter to demonstrate why and how.

My daughter enjoys great academic success which began at a very early stage. She started school at age two and a half years; and was on the honour roll in every class at every level of her learning; from kinder to primary to high school to both universities for her bachelor's and master's degrees. After reading Mike's article, I began wondering, "Could her success have resulted from me bragging about her? I've always prayed for her; as a matter of fact, when she was born I gave her back to the Lord and asked him to rear her for me. I sowed seeds for her success. I tell her constantly that she's my blessing, even now in her adult years.

I thought her blessings of success came from these spiritual actions and they do. However, this article has showed me another reason for my daughter's blessings; and that is: I tell others about her success. I tell them how I appreciate my daughter. I have a habit of telling friends that she has never let me "hold down my head," which in Jamaican parlance means "feel ashamed". We have a running joke – when I'm boasting about her in her presence, she says, "Mommy, why don't you just take your blessing and be quiet." (with a smile). She's insinuating that, at times, I don't need to brag so much.

Mike's article has also left me reflecting on a situation at my place of work. As the leader there, I faced a challenge; lack of support. This may be due to the fact that when I got the job there I "hit the ground running" trying to eliminate some behaviours I considered to be unprofessional; as well as to lift the literacy rate which was a disturbing 49%. The literacy rate did improve significantly and some of the unprofessional behaviours were eliminated in some respects.

However, in retrospect, maybe I could have done things a little differently, because although my outlook changed, there were some colleagues who still refused to catch the vision; and they were not willing to try either. Yet, I must say this kind of behaviour did not thwart my passion for the institution; neither did it affect me continuing to add value to the lives of the children and to my colleagues who had caught the vision. I looked forward to going everyday with a fresh hope that things would be different; and I believed that the change would come.

I did not feed on the negative vibes at the workplace; I considered myself a Kingdom woman; I walked with my shoulders high as if I'm a daughter of the King of Creation; I reached out to my colleagues genuinely from my heart, have apologized in instances where I've been the offender and still they refused to accept. However, I continued to pray about the situation; I had no bad intent towards any of my colleagues. I've prayed for them as I've prayed for myself.

However, and this is the challenge; based on the article, I ponder over whether I still had something to do with the lack of support. I didn't readily talk about the negative situation at the workplace and I didn't go out of my way to do so. On the other hand, I didn't brag about my colleagues either. If I was asked about the progress of the relationship there, I would say either that the situation had improved but some challenges continued; or I would mention what the challenges were; which is a form of complaining. The solution was to continue with the efforts of reaching out and when these efforts were rejected, I should do as the writer suggests, which is to continue to "honour them and their relationship to me even if I have to maintain a few boundaries;" rather than to do some form of complaining.

Another takeaway point for me is where Mike states that "honouring parents, in addition to releasing long life, releases health to both parties." My focus was usually on the promise of long life, never of health. I never interpreted "go well with thee" to mean health. Thank you for that outlook Mike.

What are your takeaway points? Note them here.

....
....
....
....
....
....
....
....
....
....
....
....
....

Again, I need to commend the Servant of God. In his sermons he has taught valuable lessons on "letting go of people" meaning that we are not to be unforgiving; but rather to "really love others, even those who might seem unlovable or who reject our love." Letting go has been so heavy on his heart that he dedicated a series of Bible study sessions on the topic 'Repentance from Deadworks;" where he stressed the need to repent; to make that turn from the deeds which cause us to be separated from God. There are times when he foregoes the sermons and engages instead in panel discussions on family life and issues, where the focus is on creating stability in the family as God ordained it; and generally imploring family members to honour each other.

I MUST HONOUR THIS SERVANT OF GOD.

11.　Honour – My Tangible Ways

Over the years, at my previous church and now at my current church at WAFIF; I've seen where I have received more as a result of being faithful and obedient to God's servant and to God Himself.

I.　TITHING

I am very serious about giving my tithes. I believe in giving back to God for what He has allowed me to have. Everything I have belongs to Him. Everything in and on the Earth is His; *"The Earth is the Lord's and the fullness thereof, the world, and they that dwell therein"***(Psalm 24:1; 1 Corinthians 10:26).**

If I might be vulnerable for a bit; in my earlier days of tithing I would divide my monthly salary into four or five parts which represented the number of weeks in a month. I'd then contribute the quarter or one fifth each Sunday. However, when I had financial challenges I'd "borrow" some money from the tithe, with the hope of replacing it before the end of the month. Sadly, on a number of occasions, I was unable to do so. Disappointment would set in; and I would make promises to myself and to my God not to repeat this wrong deed. Nonetheless, the practice continued intermittently. I knew that this was an act that went against Kingdom principles and that I would certainly miss out on my blessing – *"Bring ye all the tithes into the storehouse, that there may be meat in mine house, and prove me now herewith, saith the Lord of hosts, if I will not open* *you the windows of heaven, and pour you out a blessing, that there shall not be room enough to receive."***(Malachi 3:10 KJV).** I also learnt that if I used God's money, then an interest of 20% was due when I returned it:- *"Whoever would redeem any of their tithe must add a fifth of the value to it."***(Leviticus 27:31 NIV)**

I had to be intentional and purposeful in resisting; and to desist "borrowing" God's money. I took one tenth from my monthly salary and contributed the entire amount on one Sunday. I'd then give offerings for the other Sundays. As a matter of fact, my tithe isn't only from my salary, but from every sum of money that I receive at all times. That strategy has been successful to this day. At other times, I would sow a seed; as seen in the following Scriptures:

*"The point is this: whoever sows sparingly will also reap sparingly, and whoever sows bountifully will also reap bountifully."***(2 Corinthians 9:6 ESV);**

*"One grows freely, yet grows all the richer; another withholds what he should give, and only suffers want. Whoever brings blessing will be enriched, and one who waters will himself be watered."***(Proverbs 11:24-25 ESV).**

These are Kingdom principles friend. The more you have, the more you should give to God. The more you give to God, the better it will be for God's Servant to do the work of the Lord for the people. Your blessings will be bountiful!

II.   CHURCH PROGRAMMES

Besides tithing, there are times when God's Servant asks the believers to give towards church projects such as renovating a building or refurbishing the church yard. I freely and willingly give within my capacity. Many times it is the Lord Himself who provides the funds just in time for me to give. God is just amazing.

III.   FINANCIAL GIFT (DOUGLAS, 2012)

Always respect the principle of "double honour." There should be no special time to offer a financial gift to God's Servant. He or she is working hard in the vineyards teaching and preaching. I've given money to God's Servant out of honour. It's a Kingdom principle which has yielded amazing results. It's natural to give a financial gift at a time when the church is showing appreciation; but going the extra mile and giving a personal financial blessing which is placed into the hand of the Servant will not go unnoticed by God; *"And the first of all the first fruits of all things, and every oblation of all, of every sort of your oblations, shall be the priest's: ye shall also give unto the priest the first of your dough, that he may cause the blessing to rest in thine house"* (**Ezekiel 44:30 KJV**); and for a clearer explanation; *"The first of all the first fruits of every kind and every contribution of every kind, from all your contributions, shall be for the priests; you shall also give to the priest the first of your dough to cause a blessing to rest on your house."*(**Ezekiel 44:30 NASB**)

IV. MISCELLANEOUS GIFT

It should become natural to offer a gift to God's Servant, the spouse or the children. Gifts of clothing, jewellery, books, fruits, vegetables; even a pack of peanuts, will be appreciated. It's a wonderful habit to take a gift when you are going to see God's Chief Servant for a personal meeting. It's been a pleasure for me to do this; it gives a wonderful feeling inside. Such gestures show honour and by extension God is honoured. The various expressions on the faces of the children when gifts are given are unforgettable.

V. MISCELLANEOUS ACTIVITIES

This one gives me great pleasure, especially for the children of God's servants. Taking them on a trip, taking them for lunch, helping with homework or school work, tying shoe laces, listening to stories about their pets or school; taking pictures of them with their pets; taking pictures of them having fun; helping them to prepare for activities and other things pay dividends. Children having fun is a blessing; and being the facilitator of that fun is an honour showed to them and to God. This gift is also reciprocal because I too receive honour from God.

VI. CHURCH FUNCTIONS

Whenever there are appreciation functions for God's Servants; I try to be present or to assist if asked to serve. This shows honour. I also try to be present at Bible study, church services, members meetings and others which require my presence. I try not to be too complacent, or yield to feelings of tiredness caused by my day to day activities. As a matter of fact, I've never felt too tired to go the church or to do the activities required; and I hope I never will. Being present, shows that I appreciate God's Servant and that I believe the Word that he shares is from God. God's Servant is anointed; and listening to his teachings and preaching gives me more.

VII.   PRAYERS(DOUGLAS, 2012)

OH, I pray for the Man of God, his wife and his children often, if not daily. I am also grateful for the character of this Chief Servant, who humbly and constantly asks us to pray for him. One of the mistakes believers make is to assume that the Man of God does not need prayers. Also it would amount to folly for any Servant of God to believe that he or she does not need prayers. In fact, this amounts to arrogance. The Apostle Paul asked for prayers. Whenever he did so, I believe he was not only asking for prayers for his team of Apostles; but for intercession for all who are in ministry doing the work of God. **(2 Thessalonians 3:1-2, Colossians 4:2-3, 1Timothy 2:1-4).**

The Man of God occupies a position that puts him in the firing range of the enemy, he battles against strongholds which are bitterly opposed to the service that he has been commissioned to render. Also, the Man of God first and foremost is human; he suffers and experiences the same emotional challenges that all humans experience **(James 5:12, 2 Cor 7: 5-7),** but he is kept by the grace of the One who has called him into service. Paul was hindered in his ministry on many occasions by Satan. Peter was also thrown into jail because of the gospel and it took the intercession of the believers to deliver them. **(Acts 12:5-11, 2 Corinthians 12:7)**(Bolaji 'Theo' Douglas)

VIII.   OBEDIENCE(DOUGLAS, 2012)

There are a variety of things the Man of God asks our church to do, including, a 21-day fast; a weekly 24 hour fast; sowing a seed; doing 10 days of prayer to seek the filling of the Holy Spirit, making a pledge toward a specific church project, assisting our fellow church members financially or otherwise; and more. I try to obey gladly and willingly. I do so because it's also a requirement of the people of God. *"Obey your spiritual leaders, and do what they say. Their work is to watch over your souls, and they are accountable to God. Give them reason to do this with joy and not with sorrow: that would certainly not be for your benefit"***(Hebrews 13:17 NLT).** At times, the Man of God may be heard saying, "When you don't do your part in obedience, it makes my work harder; it becomes stressful."

The Servant of God should never have to resort to this; to feeling overwhelmed and overworked; because as the Word says, it won't benefit you, the believer.

12.   Honour – Personal Rewards

In giving honour, I have reaped personally. As stated earlier, it's a Kingdom principle. If you honour, you WILL be honoured; there are no two ways about it; it MUST happen! It WILL happen! *"If you want to be loved, give love to others. If you want honour live an honourable life and bestow honour unto others. If your desire is to financially prosper, plant seeds of finances. Whatsoever you sow and cultivate is the fruit you will reap."*(Roden)

As a result of living a life committed to tithing and sowing; I have reaped rewards, to which I owe a debt of gratitude to my Heavenly Father; and for which I give Him thanks daily. These rewards are not limited to but include:

I.   DEBT REDUCTION

I smile, cry, laugh, boast about God's goodness; or just, as Mary, the Mother of my Lord did, quietly ponder in my heart; when I remember this awesome Act of God. It started with being severely financially strapped. This was as a result of sacrificing for my daughter's education after she was successful in gaining entry into Columbia University, in the United States, to complete her 'Master in Screen Writing and Directing'. I'm getting goose pimples just reliving this in writing. The second income earmarked to be used to finance this loan; became nonexistent after HOT 102, the radio station to which I was employed, folded due to financial challenges. The size of the loan may be deduced from the comment of the Loans Manager at the bank from which I received the loan. He said that none of their clients had ever taken a loan that size for education; but rather for opening a business, purchasing a house or purchasing a vehicle. He commended me for this feat and assured me that it was greatly appreciated by my daughter and that the benefits would be returned.

Well, I was not able to repay after months of losing that second income. In summary, what happened was that my house was advertised in the newspaper for the first of three times; the third time would have caused me to lose it completely since that's when houses are placed on the auction block. Friend, please believe me when I say that I was not perturbed. I remember being happy that my daughter was not in Jamaica to experience any embarrassment which could arise from this grave occurrence. I began wondering where would I go? Who would I ask to store my furniture? I am from a very small family; and my uncle couldn't help. Relatives were out of the question; and I am of the firm belief that good friends cease being that when they have to make such a huge sacrifice for you. So how was this to be solved?

All through that time, I prayed consistently. The bank couldn't help me anymore; neither could the professional Association to which I had membership; nor my Credit Union; although the latter made representations on my behalf to the bank's lawyers. Nothing was forthcoming. However, I stood on the promises of God; I continued to be obedient in giving tithes and I sowed my financial seeds from my first income, even in my deep financial woes. I expected a miracle; MY MIRACLE! God promised me through His Word when It states, *"Give, and you will receive. Your gift will return to you in full—pressed down, shaken together to make room for more, running over, and poured into your lap. The amount you give will determine the amount you get back."***(Luke 6:38 NLT);** and *"Be not deceived; God is not mocked: for whatsoever a man soweth, that shall he also reap."***(Galatians 6:7 KJV).** Also, *"The LORD himself goes before you and will be with you; He will never leave you nor forsake you. Do not be afraid; do not be discouraged."***(Galatians 6:7 ERV).** I fed upon these Words and I patiently waited, knowing that God would come through with my financial miracle.

In summary, one day I received a call from the manager of my Credit Union. She was also a mighty woman of God. She stated that the lawyer had decided to write off half a million dollars from my loan; just like that! I didn't have to do anything. It just happened! My debt had been reduced! Her loans' officer, through whom I did the initial business, was baffled and stated that in all her years working at the credit union, she had not experienced that phenomenon. She was baffled! I was not! My God had come through for me as I knew He would. The Credit Union was able to take over the loan from the bank. I continued to service that loan but it became more bearable. God eased the burden; He said, *"For my yoke is easy and my burden is light."***(Matthew 11:30 NIV).** I sowed and I reaped. To God be the Glory!

Other financial breakthroughs include finding pounds (British currency), sent to me for Christmas or for my birthday (I can't remember), by my mom and which I had put away because I didn't have an immediate need at the time. I forgot about this money. The story is that I thought I was flat broke. My car insurance was due and there was no money to pay. With tears, I started searching everywhere in my house. Somehow I knew my God would come through in some way; my human thoughts could not perceive how, but I knew it was possible! *"For nothing will be impossible with God"***(Luke 1:37 NASB).** I found the money in the envelope as it had come, in a dresser drawer. The equivalent in Jamaican currency, turned out to be the exact amount I needed to pay the insurance. The song, 'My God is an Awesome God" comes to mind. God is indeed awesome!

When my daughter started her first degree at Ryerson University in Toronto; things became grave financially and we were not able to pay her tuition a few times. There was one time in particular when they proposed to send her back to Jamaica with all the support possible to enable her to continue her studies at the University. A number of things happened. I prayed from my corner of the world while she, having become the mature individual that studying overseas and having the right ambition allow you to be; made representations to the financial staff at her university. What happened was that God inspired and God favoured. The University would alert her to grants which were available; she was allowed to work while studying; and then she received a huge scholarship which would take care of all her finances for the duration of her studies. That scholarship also allowed payment of her airfare back to Jamaica on completion of her degree. That was favour! We had received our blessing from the Lord! She graduated with honours and with all her lecturers wanting to meet the mother of this outstanding student. I planted seeds of finance and the favour was returned!

Through my giving financially, my daughter has received job offers consistently; as soon as one project is completed, she receives another offer and each comes with a pay cheque which surpasses the previous one. In one instance, she received an offer that came while she was engaged in a project for only six weeks. She took the offer as the financial reward surpassed what she was receiving at the time. God keeps bettering his blessings and favour. The wonderful thing is, based on the blessing upon my life through my giving to the Lord, my daughter has also become consistent in giving her tithes as well. Her act of giving back to the Lord, has also caused the financial breakthroughs in her life.

As mentioned earlier, "If your desire is to financially prosper, plant seeds of finances."

II. THE ANOINTING

In addition to the financial benefits, honouring God's Chief Servant, Bishop Courtney McLean, has afforded me the joy of receiving an anointing that has been on his life as well. You will remember his pronouncement upon me; "Everything I have I give to you." I received that anointing in faith. Out of that blessing, God has given me the inspiration to write this book and to have two or three other books within me, which will become realities sooner than later. I am also "kicking" the procrastination habit which has been plaguing me for years. Bishop McLean is a man on the move; he does what he has to do tirelessly. He said I have the strength and I should JUST DO IT!

Now, I've made the effort toward opening my own Literacy business and office which I have been neglecting to do for at least 10 years. Also, after declining speaking engagements for years; until people stopped making requests; I have decided to accept once again and for the graduation season of 2017, I endorsed and committed to speak at two events. Furthermore, I now have the zeal to do specific activities including facilitating personal and professional development seminars locally. I also attended the prestigious well respected IMC, International Maxwell Certification Conference in August 2017 in Orlando. John Maxwell is arguably the top leadership guru in the world. This is huge. It was a big risk; a heavy sacrifice but it happened. Bishop McLean is an author; has started his business; is a certified Maxwell coach and speaker; and frequently does motivational speaking to churches and other organizations. Under the anointing, my latent gift has been realized as well; I too am a John Maxwell Team member, I'm mentoring; coaching and masterminding; training managers in companies; and generally adding value to people's lives. To God be the glory!

In addition, as I reflect on how favoured I am as a result of honouring God and His Chief Servant; my mind goes back to the fact that in 2016 between March and December, I travelled overseas three times, all gratis; first to Orlando to Disney World; then to Miami for my past student's graduation from University; as well as to Toronto to spend Christmas with my daughter.

III. ARMOUR OF GOD

Honouring has caused me over the years to remain steadfast in overcoming the battles with principalities and powers, spiritual wickedness in high places, and against the rulers of this dark world, when they surfaced at my workplace via my own colleagues. Then there's the situation with the parent, the details of which I will not include here, as it was told in an earlier chapter, but it was God's Chief Servant who had given me a Word that helped me to win against the demon which tried to land me in court innocently.

There are other personal life changing events but the foregoing gives an idea of the tremendous benefits that may be received simply by doing as God mandates; and that is honouring God and His Servant who is toiling for our souls. With some of these tangible blessings, to which I refer as rewards for my honouring, I now stand to earn more financially, doing the things I enjoy and moving towards realizing the prophetic destiny ordained by my Creator. It is my view that these experiences are not unique to me. They result from giving honour to whom it is due, namely God Almighty and His Servants.

13.   Honour - Suggestions

In this closing chapter, I would like to make some suggestions which I will call Spiritual Mathematical Reasoning. As was stated earlier, "If you want to be loved, give love to others. If you want honour live an honourable life and bestow honour unto others. If your desire is to financially prosper, plant seeds of finances. Whatsoever you sow and cultivate is the fruit you will reap."

It stands to reason then, that the following suggestions may just work:

- If, for whatever reason, you are having difficulty adding a child to the family, may I suggest honouring some persons by volunteering in a children's home, mentoring or fostering a child or assisting a family in caring for a child or children

- If you have challenges with your health, volunteer at a hospital; assist a sick friend in filling hospital appointments or with purchasing medicines if there's a challenge. Also pray for the sick although you might be sick.

- Not much food in your cupboard? Share the little that you have with someone; maybe at a home for the elderly, a homeless person on the street, one of those windscreen wipers (although you may have to be careful in some respects) or your next door neighbour who might be in need. Remember the story of the Widow of Zarephath and Elijah? She had what she considered her last meal which, according to her, she was going to prepare for herself and her son and then die. Elijah advised her to prepare the meal and offer to him first then prepare for herself and her son. She honoured Elijah. She obeyed; and the amount which would have constituted her last meal was shared for Elijah, for her and her son; and lasted for many days. **(1 Kings 17:7-16)**

- If you know that your Servant of God is leading a miracle and deliverance service; and you are in need of a miracle or deliverance; go in faith and become a part of the atmosphere. As God moves through His servant and miracles are worked, honour God's servant or the person who received the miracle; so the anointing may also fall on you to receive your own miracle. **"Often time the breakthrough that we need rests on someone" (Roy Roden).** He further states that we can obtain the breakthrough that we need by honouring that person. It's a Kingdom principle. You draw the anointing of another by your honour to that person. Remember, "*For the measure you give will be the measure you get back.*"**(Luke 6:38 NRSV).** Also, remember that "*the testimony of Jesus is the spirit of prophecy*"**(Revelations 19:10 KJV).** When your colleague testifies about a miracle which you also need, that is the time to receive your miracle as well; as the atmosphere is ripe for you to do so; the portals of heaven open for you.

There is one drawback from receiving the breakthrough though. Your honour of someone has to come from a clean and genuine heart. Jesus called those who honoured Him with their lips and not their hearts; hypocrites. **(Matthew 15:7-8)**

14. The End

What a pleasure it has been paying honour to one who truly deserves it! This Chief Servant of God, this Shepherd, Bishop Courtney McLean has worked tirelessly among the sheep; sometimes emptying himself for the work of the Lord. I have experienced where it became normal for this Servant to do a Facebook Live session at 5:00 o'clock on a Sunday morning; and then travelled to WAFIF to deliver three sermons at 7:00 a.m.; 9:00 a.m.; and 11:00 a.m. Then sometimes between two services, when he should be refreshing himself in preparation for the next service, he would pop in to 'Facebook Live' just to assure the members and visitors of God's love for them and encourage them to remain faithful to the God of all Gods. What a Servant!

The demand for audience with him is great because people realize that there's something special about this servant. He works tirelessly for the Kingdom; and I am grateful to God for having connected me to Bishop McLean and to the brethren at WAFIF. It's been a wonderful spirit-filled experience so far; and it can only get better because I plan to push harder and follow hard after God. It is God's desire for me and I have a spiritual father who considers it his calling to steer his sheep in like direction.

Let me pause here to say that showing honour to Bishop McLean by producing this book should not be seen as a unique exercise. I'm doing this because of my personal need to do so; based on my experience with this Servant of God; and based on the tremendous blessing which I have received. However, I believe I'm also sending a message to you if you're a believer; to endeavour to show honour to your Chief Servant. I have chosen to do a book, among other things, as seen within the chapters. What are you going to do?

There are a few things to consider:

(i) Are you a Believer? (I hope you are. That's the only way to be saved **(Acts 16:31);** and not be condemned **(John 3:18).**

(ii) Are you connected to a house of worship? (I hope you are. God delights in a house built to worship Him. He fills it with His glory **(Exodus 40:34)**, and calls it a house of prayer for all people **(Isaiah 56:7)**

(iii) Are you getting vital, spiritual food from your Chief Servant? (Hopefully you are; or you need to find a house where you are fed spiritually). Your Chief Servant should be encouraging you with wholesome teaching and pointing out to you where you are wrong **(Titus 1:9).**

(iv) Do you believe the Word of God? (I hope you do.) The Word is inspired by God and equips you for every good work **(2 Timothy 3:16-17)**

All the areas above are connected. If you are a Believer, you will want to go to the house of the Lord to worship and to praise Him, to fellowship with other Believers, to feast on the Word, and to partake of the Lord's Supper. However, If you are a true Believer, you will also want to do what the Lord implores you to do; and among what the Bible teaches is that we should give double honour to those who work hard among us; especially those who preach and teach us the way to salvation. **(1Timothy 5:17).**

I am now following hard after God; I'm delving deeper into the Word, I'm more consistent, intentional and purposeful in my prayer life, I have a deep desire and a yearning to hear from the Lord, I'm no longer satisfied with this self but now have a need to be used by God. I feed my spiritual life by listening more to music and discussions that edify my soul, I sow more into the Kingdom of God and I reach out more to those who are less fortunate. I am totally sold out to Christ; I'm having FUN IN THE SON (to borrow a phrase from Tommy Cowan and Carlene Davis); and I wouldn't have it any other way at this stage of my life. These attributes have resulted in me receiving MORE. To God be the glory!

Right now I'm preoccupied with improving myself professionally so that I can continue to add value to the lives of others but in a greater way. To use an expression which is often said by my Chief Servant – "I will not die before I'm dead." I am looking forward to being used by God and to realize my prophetic destiny

This new found zeal for God has been ignited by God's Chief Servant, Bishop Courtney McLean and I thank God everyday for him; and ask the Lord to bless him and his family. I bless his wife, Reverend Nadine McLean who ably supports him so that he can give of himself to lead the sheep that God has placed in his care. I bless his children; Deborah, Dominique and

Daniel; for understanding that their daddy is also the spiritual daddy of the congregation that he leads.

Nevertheless, God's Chief Servants are everywhere; and I pray for them too that God will strengthen them and their families as they do His work across the different denominations in Jamaica, the Caribbean and the World.

So, as you read this, it is my hope that I've spurred you into reflecting on how your Chief Servant has impacted your life and the lives of your church family. I advise you to be intentional and physically note how you have changed since being connected to this Servant of God. Make a concerted effort to honour this person. You will not only be doing something worthwhile personally but you will be honouring God through honouring His Servant. Whatever, you do to the least of my brothers, Jesus said, that you do unto Him.

How will you honour your Chief Servant? It may be personal or otherwise. You may consider having a discussion with a church sister or brother who you think would be of one mind with you and together you plan something. You could be bold enough and get a group of persons involved. Whatever it is, do something; lead the way. I'm mindful of the fact that many churches have Appreciation ceremonies for their leaders and everybody is encouraged to participate, and they usually do as best as they can. However, based on the impact your Chief Servant has had on you personally, you might want to extend yourself to a greater level just to show your personal appreciation. Just ensure that it comes from the heart and not done to "show off" or "show up" anyone. Remember, honouring

God's Chief Servant is honouring God and God cannot be mocked.

So, go ahead, make a list of a number of ways you can show your honour to God's Chief Servant and do it. You will be held in high esteem by the Almighty God. You will be tremendously blessed. God, the Creator, who owns the heavens and the Earth and all that is in it **(Psalm 24:1);** the God who owns the cattle on a thousand hills **(Psalm 50:10)**; God who owns the treasures of darkness and hidden riches of secret places **(Isaiah 45:3)** will honour you! You will receive the MORE that you have been hoping for.

APPENDIX 1

Mike Phillips is a writer, speaker, pastor and counsellor, ordained and licensed pastor with the Christian and Missionary Alliance, both in Canada and the United States, where he was pastor for four churches for over 36 years. Mike has also worked with churches and groups in the Assembly of God, Foursquare and Vineyard movements. Mike and his wife Kathy spent many years in pastoral ministry working with churches that had fallen apart and needed to be rebuilt.

In 1999, they moved to Sacramento, CA to plant Gateway Fellowship Church. In August of 2015, Mike left Gateway to pursue a broader ministry spectrum through writing, counselling and speaking. In addition to his work as pastor, Mike also ministers to missionaries in many organizations. Primarily, he has served with Youth with a Mission, teaching over 90 schools in the past 24 years. He focuses on topics such as "Hearing God's Voice", "Healing from Your Past" and "Prayer and Intercession."

Mike's degrees are in Theology and Counselling and he has done extensive work utilizing Memory Processing, TPM, Myers-Briggs Indicator, Choice/Reality Therapy and Life Coaching. He brings all of this experience into his writing and speaking. Mike continues to keep a full counselling load and even does 6-10 hours a week of counselling online through Skype and Face time. He specializes in post-traumatic stress, addiction, eating disorders, self-harm, sexual dysfunction, anger management, loss of reality and depression.

Mike has published four books and 97 articles with Christian magazines such as Christianity Today, Leadership, Charisma, Computing Today and Alliance Life. His book on parenting ("To Be A Father Like the Father") sold 20,000 copies and was on the Christian book bestseller list for four months.

Mike's current book is called "The Spirit Walk" and became available in the summer of 2016.

Mike has a wife, Kathy, and three children, John, Andrew, and Meaghan. He currently lives in Sacramento, California when he is not traveling for speaking and counselling ministry

DECLARATION OF HONOUR

I believe in the Chief Servant with whom God has connected me. I will be obedient to this Servant. I will honour him/her and I will prosper in every area of my life.

Bible Translations

KJV   King James Version

NLT   New Living Translation

NASB   New American Standard Bible

ESV   English Standard Version

NIV   New International Version

GW   God's Word Translation

ASV   American Standard Version

AMP   Amplified Bible

ERV   Holy Bible: Easy to Read Version

NRSV   New Revised Standard Version

REFERENCES

Douglas, B. ". (2012, May 2). *Teachings & Sermons*. Retrieved February 20, 2017, from The Bread From Heaven Ministries: http://www.thebreadfromheaven.com/index.php?option =com_content&view=article&id=200:honouring-the-man-of-god-&catid=53:the-church-of-christ&Itemid=54

Honour God. (n.d.). Retrieved February 20, 2017, from Got Questions? Kidz: http://www.gqkidz.org/honor-God.html

Roden, R. (n.d.). *Journals*. Retrieved June 18, 2017, from Destiny East Gate Ministries: http://www.destinyeastgateministries.org/journals/pro phetic-tidbits/the-power-of-honor/

The Danger of Dishonour. (2013, September 23). Retrieved February 20, 2017, from The Gates Are Open: https://natomaschurch.wordpress.com/2013/09/23/th e-danger-of-dishonor

Vasu, D. S. (2007, February 4). *The Danger of Dishonouring God's Anointed People*. Retrieved February 20, 2017, from Sermon Central: February 4, 2007, retrieved February 20, 2017, https://www.sermoncentral.com/sermons/the-danger-of-dishonouring-gods-anointed-people-dr-stanley-vasu-sermon-on-christian-disciplines-102068?page=4

WikiHow. (n.d.). *WikiHow to do anything... WikiHow to Honour God*. Retrieved February 20, 2017, from Honour God serving Others: http://www.wikihow.com/honor-God#Serving_Others_sub

Wikipedia. (2017, April 24). *Cursillo*. Retrieved June 18, 2017, from Wikipedia: https://en.wikipedia.org/wiki/Cursillo

ABOUT THE AUTHOR

*Thelma Porter is currently in Educational Leadership as the principal in the primary school system in St. Andrew; Jamaica. She's a coach, speaker and trainer with the John Maxwell Team having become certified in August 2017. She credits John Maxwell and her spiritual father, Bishop Courtney McLean as her inspiration for writing this book. She however has two previous publications to her credit; including **Making Learning 'Cool' By Making the Environment Creatively Real and Interesting** found in Journal of Best Practices in Teaching and Learning; and **Learner Processes, Teacher Processes and the Development of Learner Abilities**.*

She is a Christian who has served in leadership roles in various church ministries; and thrives on building the Kingdom of God by adding value to the lives of those with whom she comes in contact. She believes this book will further advance that cause as there are tried and proven principles that will assist the believer and nonbeliever alike. She currently heads the Communications Ministry at Worship and Faith International Fellowship, her church home.

She has served in other leadership roles in the secular world including the PR Chairperson for the Jamaica Teachers' Association; Community Representative on the board of the Richmond Park Basic School and member of the National Council on Education in Jamaica; Her achievements include the Mico University College's 175th Anniversary Award for Distinguished

Service to Education; the JTA Award for Conference year 2013-2014; and several certificates for leadership training since 2013.

She is the Proprietor of The Growth Institute and thrives by the philosophies "Seek value, get value, give value"; and "Work hard to save one, and save more". Thelma Porter has used these models to facilitate the change she wants to see in herself; and as leader, teacher, coach and speaker; she has seen God transform the mindsets and attitudes of many individuals, through her intervention in their lives.

www.ingramcontent.com/pod-product-compliance
Lightning Source LLC
Chambersburg PA
CBHW060357050426
42449CB00009B/1780